THE NOT-RIGHT HOUSE
ESSAYS ON JAMES PURDY

THE NOT-RIGHT HOUSE

Essays on James Purdy

by

BETTINA SCHWARZSCHILD

Missouri Literary Frontiers Series Number 5
UNIVERSITY OF MISSOURI PRESS
COLUMBIA • MISSOURI

For Arthur
and to Edith Weiss
with thanks

INTRODUCTION

Approximately a dozen years ago when I was book editor of a newspaper with a shall we say very modest circulation, there turned up on my desk two small paperbound books written and illustrated by an American author I had never heard of (the books, he was to tell me some years later, had been printed for private distribution by two friends, Osborn Andreas and J. J. Sjoblom, residents of Chicago). One of the little books (it contained sixty-nine pages) was a novella which began:

> 'Do you ever think about Fenton Riddleway?' Parkhearst Cratty asked the greatwoman when they were sitting in the summer garden of her 'mansion.'
>
> Although the greatwoman had been drinking earlier in the day, she was almost sober at the time Parkhearst put this question to her.

The other paperback was somewhat larger, ninety-one pages, and consisted of nine stories, only three of which had been previously published. Neither book, to the best of my knowledge, received much attention, critical or otherwise, but then neither did *Tales of the Grotesque and Arabesque* or *Dubliners* and more than a few other books which subsequently became classics. Finally, though, they were published commercially in England with the titles *63: Dream Palace* and later, in the late fall of 1957, in America as *Color of Darkness*. The rest, of course, is literary history.

Though none of James Purdy's works of fiction have been commercially successful, his reputation has grown steadily with each subsequent book (the novels *Malcolm*, 1959, *The*

Nephew, 1960, *Cabot Wright Begins*, 1964, *Eustace Chisholm and the Works*, 1967, and a second collection of stories and two plays, *Children is All*, 1962). *63: Dream Palace* and at least one of his novels are indisputably contemporary classics; his stories have been anthologized time and time again; his plays have been produced in Germany and Jugoslavia; his works have been translated into more than a score of languages including Chinese; critics increasingly reckon him as one of the major writers of our times. A quiet, contemplative man who avoids publicity and looks upon the cocktail-and-television-appearances circuit of the New York publishing world as one of the many manifestations of Hell in contemporary society, Purdy at forty-five lives and writes in comparative isolation, a reject, in his own words, from a sick society.

It is as a prose poet of the grotesque and the alienated, as I have commented elsewhere, that Purdy has achieved his highest success. His is a strange and highly individual talent. He is preoccupied with the paradoxes he finds in the human situation — love-hate, beauty-ugliness, compassion-cruelty. He leads us into a world in which customary values are reversed, where the familiar suddenly becomes terrifying, as though one walking through a well-known terrain were to find himself at the edge of a void alive with sights and sounds only partly recognizable.

Bettina Schwarzschild's essays help us see this strange world afresh. She has read Purdy with wisdom and insight. She understands his exiled wanderers perhaps more thoroughly than any one else who has written of them, knows that to love them means to be shaken with pity and terror. So, of course, does their creator.

WILLIAM PEDEN

THE NOT-RIGHT HOUSE

James Purdy with a Christian vision of love tells in *63: Dream Palace* the story of "the least among us," Fenton Riddleway, "dumb and innocent and getting to be mad," and his little brother Claire, helpless, puny and seemingly feebleminded. To love them means to be shaken with pity and terror. It means to know utter despair, for there is nothing anyone can do to save them. They are doomed.

The "least" in Purdy's work is the exiled wanderer, abandoned in a strange world where nothing makes sense, where he can find no hold. Once he leaves his natural home, the golden bench of Malcolm, the West Virginia farm of Fenton, or Cousin Ida's cottage of Amos Ratcliffe, he is Ulysses faced with monsters at every turn. But unlike Ulysses, he cannot slay them. If he is like Bennie of "Daddy Wolf," with no money to spend, he doesn't even rate a perforation on the program card. His auditors accuse him of lacking an indefinable something, of not having what it takes. What he lacks is the ability to be non-human. His humanity is his Achilles heel. He limps through life bleeding with every step he takes.

A father or a Mr. Kincaid has left this orphaned transient in a hotel room or directed him to a condemned, rotting slum house. He is supposed to return and show the youth how to go on from there, but he never does. Waiting for father turns into waiting for death.

Lost in the disintegrating "not-right house," as Fenton calls it, without guidebook or knowledge of the language spoken, the exile drifts like a shade in hell:

> That was why the big old house with tall rooms was getting more ghostly for him, it was so much like the way

1

he was inside himself, the house didn't work at all, and he was all stopped inside himself too just like the house. That was why it was like a trap.

Fenton asks, "Do you really think we're *in* the right house maybe?" With terror he realizes that this is the only house there is. He is trapped in a not-right body, not-right house, and not-right world.

And still the forsaken son waits and dreams of the father who will mend *the damage in the machinery of the cosmos*, as the not-right human condition is called in *Malcolm*, and of a father who says, "You are my son, today I have begotten you." (Psalm II). The recognition and acceptance of his begetter would give the child a sense of belonging and reality. Without it he is the sperm that got away, the bedbug crawling on Claire's cot.

Not every son waits passively for his abdicated father. Cabot Wright avenges the abandonment by assaulting the idols and sacred cows of "The not-right house." "Marriages were broken up by him. . . . Nothing was ever the same after Cabot Wright left." Cabot is the mythical hero, the abandoned child destined to kill his unknown father and all the institutions of the establishment that are a part of his begetter's life.

When the father *is* present, he is so ineffectual and impotent that the son could not feel more forsaken if he were left in the wilderness to perish. This kind of desertion too is avenged in Purdy's work. Baxter of "Color of Darkness" kicks the father in the groin, who feels nausea at the word *son*, and Bobby Zeller of "Cutting Edge" contemptuously parades naked in front of his irresponsible parents.

In *Eustace Chisholm and The Works*, the father suddenly appears after fifteen years at the scene of his careless crime, and instead of initiating his son into manhood, he mutilates him with castrating words. Mortally wounded, Amos says, "Go back and put your condoms on the line to dry." This bitter retort contains the horror and sense of insignificance of the

2

child who knows he was unwilled by his father, an escapee from the condom that perhaps had been used on another woman before his mother. "I could be any man's son," he declares.

In the absence of the begetter, every man the boy meets becomes his father, and each man in turn becomes a deserter. For Malcolm it is Mr. Cox, Girard, and Gus. For Amos Ratcliffe it is Daniel and the frivolous playboy, Reuben Masterson, of whom Amos says, "I've become the child Reuben Masterson had to give birth to, and it's no surprise therefore he's deposited me with his Grandmother while the heir and father goes scot free to worship Bacchus."

The wanderer is destroyed in a loveless, fatherless world, but if he stays home he is devoured by the mother who loves him too much. Either way he is doomed. And so is the mother. In "Children is All" and "Eventide," she is asked to give up what was once a part of her body. But love seeks union and not separation. For the mother the machinery of the cosmos has been damaged, too. When civilization started with consciousness and subsequently the incest taboo, tragedy came into the world, and *she* was the first victim.

If the mother keeps her son she suffocates him and if she lets him go, heroically, she abandons him to the hounds. Life is full of such impossible alternatives, enacted comically in "Don't Call Me By My Right Name" and tragically in *Eustace Chisholm and The Works*. In "Sound of Talking," Mrs. Farebrother hurts her husband by not looking at his crippled legs and hurts him when she does. She is reduced to a life of furtive glances, as trapped as her husband in the wheelchair. Nothing we do is right, the author tells us relentlessly. "You have no choice but to make mistakes," the speaker says in "Sermon."

But Purdy's exiles pay no attention to the "Sermon." They go on longing for the "right-house" where no mistakes are made.

3

"Many of you feel there must be a better place for you than the one you are occupying now. There is a feeling of everything being not quite right. You feel if you only knew more or could do more you would be somewhere else." ("Sermon")

But when Mrs. Farebrother stopped wanting to be somewhere else she was dead:

Then suddenly she knew she wanted nothing. She did not believe anybody could give her anything. One thing or another or nothing were all the same.

Purdy's anguished people are being kept alive by an undercurrent of yearning, yearning for immortality, eternal youth, a reward for life, the return of a dead son or timeless love: "everything under the sun." The longing to be God, omniscient and immortal, drives Captain Stadger (*Eustace Chisholm and The Works*), to pierce the innermost being of Daniel Haws, where he thinks the secret is lodged. Failure maddens him with despair and he shoots himself.

Purdy's wanderers rarely kill themselves though. They endure. They are like Lafe in "You Reach for Your Hat" of whom his war widow says:

"He never was a real lively one, but he had a kind of hard enduring quality in him that must have been hard to put out. He must have died slow and hard and knowing to the end."

And they are like Bennie of "Daddy Wolf," who holds on when there is nothing to hold on to. His last link with the world is the "trouble phone" in the hallway of his rat infested tenement in "the not-right house." When he is disconnected from the stranger he picked at random he pleads with the operator, "Just connect me back, will you please. This here is an emergency phone call."

Purdy's "disconnected" people stagger through life with an

incurable sense of loss borne in quiet desperation. Yet at the same time, in a secret chamber of their heart, remains a belief in the pot of gold, no matter how much daily evidence there is to the contrary.

The madness of this yearning is illustrated by the grandfather in "Home by Dark," who tells his grandson, "There is always one thing a person believes, and wants to believe, even if he doesn't believe it." The little boy wants to believe that his dead parents can be alive again. This yearning lays bare a sorrow and sense of loss so great that the loving grandfather cannot listen to it. Perceptive, the child then says, "Well let's talk about things we can tell each other." At that moment a wall has been erected between the old man and the child that isolates them both.

In their isolation, the exiles have a yearning to penetrate this wall through love. How they hunger for this love! Even promiscuous Carrie Moore (*Cabot Wright Begins*) craves something beyond orgasm. In her frequent changes of husbands and bedmates she is looking for love. This yearning is a hunger of the soul.

Though Purdy's hungry exiles must have love to survive, they run from it like the plague. It's too painful to love the "least" as the grandfather of "Home by Dark" showed. "If bodies are united by pleasure, souls are united by pain." (Unamuno). Daniel Haws thought he could escape this pain. But the soul does not surrender without a battle and release from its pain has to be earned, he discovers, with disembowelment.

The exiled wanderers in James Purdy's work, lost in the unnatural world, seek a hold on their strange surroundings, which no one has taught them how to obtain. They pour themselves out, sparing no unacceptable detail, revealing what we are most ashamed of, with the immediacy of Bennie's "emergency phone call." ("Daddy Wolf.") Through them James Purdy relates how mankind was cast out of the womb of

5

nature, "the right house," and abandoned by its begetter to primal solitude. He tells of helpless, bewildered man, "eating the bitter bread of banishment," (Richard II) and of the wanderer's longing for a protecting father and of his yearning to return home. Humanity's biography is told through the artist's rich imagery, primordial and ever new.

FENTON RIDDLEWAY: *63: Dream Palace*

December Magazine, Vol. VIII, No. 1, 1966

In "You Reach For Your Hat," Mamie, the small-town widow, has come to Jennie whose young soldier husband was killed in the war, for a "sweet memory talk" — the sentimental things we say about the dead — and instead she's forced to listen to the unspeakable truth. She cries out, "You've said such awful things tonight. . . . Leave me my little mental comforts." It's a moment when we see life with its rooted sorrow and absurdity that has nothing in common with the slick, glossy bill of goods the advertisers sell us. James Purdy is no advertiser, no seducer coaxing us with sweet memory talks and little mental comforts. He puts his finger on our psychic wounds and it hurts to the quick. With this preparation we descend into the subworld of *63: Dream Palace.*

The story has the deceptive simplicity and inevitability of a folk myth, which indeed it is. Fenton Riddleway explains in one breath:

> . . . that he was Fenton Riddleway and that he was nineteen, that he had come with his brother Claire from West Virginia, from a town near Ronceverte, that their mother had died two weeks before and that a friend of his named Kincaid had given him an address in a rooming house on Sixty-three Street. . . .

It turns out to be a "not-right kind of place" at all "that has survived by oversight." In this house, where Claire hears voices of God or ghosts, they find a bug-ridden, dwarf-sized cot on which both brothers take turn sleeping.

Fenton Riddleway is lost in the park and is looking for the exit. "Everything about him was too large for him, the speech, the terrible clothes, the ragged hair, the possible gun, the outlandish accent." Nothing fits. He is the castaway orphaned misfit who has left his bucolic home and is afloat in the asphalt jungle. He is the "marginal" American who just wants to get by and finds it impossible.

James Purdy then tells us in a hushed voice of the utter indifference of the city to the dead shades "wandering away from the light," and the young boys with the look of caged tigers, "dumb and innocent and getting to be mad." They drift into the streets "where no one really belonged or stayed very long," in unnumbered houses which "look so rotten and devoured that you can't believe they were ever built. . . ." He tells of the city of all-night taverns and all-night movie theaters where the same sickly smelling vagrants sleep that can be found on the pavement outside; of the city where the forces of violence begrudge Fenton Riddleway the little he asks and the corruptors under the guise of benevolence insist that he ask for more.

James Purdy has a gift for making places and objects spring to life in the primeval, animistic way of great poets. Seats of the movie theater "do not act as if they were required to hold you off the floor," buildings lean forward "as if to bend down to the street," the silence of the city at night has "many little contractions and movements like the springs of a poorly constructed machine," and the "not-right house" on 63 Street "is all stuffed up" and somehow gives the eerie feeling that anyone entering it will never leave, dead or alive.

Parkhearst Cratty, a writer manqué, meets Fenton Riddleway while wandering in the park looking for material for a book, which he'll never write, of course, as he is looking in the wrong place. The artist must look into himself for in-

7

spiration. Besides, his first artistic creation is himself, as Otto Rank has said, and Parkhearst Cratty on the contrary has destroyed himself. Demanding that something should happen, he cries out for a reward, "A reward for life just as I have lived it." In answer life sends him Fenton Riddleway. It is the only reward life has, "just as he has lived it." His past. There is "a wildness and freedom about Fenton Riddleway" that stirs up memories of a former self, before Cratty became a kept man. The memory makes him acutely sick. He must destroy Fenton the way he was destroyed by luring him into the vampire's lair.

Parkhearst Cratty brings him to the mansion of Grainger, the greatwoman. Coming from the rotting house into the greatwoman's mansion, Fenton observes that "It was almost as dark . . . as the house where he and Claire had been waiting, the ceiling was no taller." In a brilliant flash we see that there is little difference between the rotting house and the mansion. They are both "not-right houses," places where you wait — wait for it all to end. Fenton Riddleway waits with the desperation of a trapped animal, knowing all along that "nobody was ever coming to the house because it was the latest time in life." When in this utter hopeless situation help is offered, help with strings attached by corrupting hands, he knows this is how it has to be. "Well, when there ain't nothing, you got to stoop down and pick up the rotten." If Fenton Riddleway accepts the "rotten," he too will become Parkhearst Cratty, a rich woman's lapdog. But if he does not, at best he will live the life of a slum rat.

The drunken woman in the mansion, called Grainger or greatwoman, has eyes ". . . blackened very little with mascara and yet such was their cavernous appearance they gaped at Parkhearst as though tonight they would yield him her real identity and why people called her great."

To the semi-barbaric country boy of West Virginia, as she sits, "raised on a little platform in a mammoth chair," she looks beautiful like a princess in an old story book. She is the fairy princess, bestower of gifts. But when she offers Fenton Riddleway a gift too many, her dead husband's garments, she becomes Jocasta giving the young Oedipus the mantle of Laius, and then we see her through the eyes of her emasculated cohort, Parkhearst Cratty, as "The Queen of Hell." She *is* "more than a human personage," Persephone and Aphrodite both, giver and taker of life—primeval mother of us all. To Fenton Riddleway and Parkhearst Cratty, heirs to this archetypal vision, she is the *greatwoman.*

Commenting on James Purdy's uncanny insight into woman, the poet John Cowper Powys and psychologist Edmond Bergler, among others, marveled at how one so young knew so much. If the primitive mind is in the fullest meaning of the word imperishable, as Freud said, then we are all born with the image of woman that primitive man revered and feared: The great mother—giver of life and death, Queen Isis, *known by many names.* To most of us the door of this cave knowledge closes in early childhood, and the creatures behind this door make themselves visible only in our dreams. But to the artist the door remains open. He captures this vision and transforms it into a living monument. Combine this access to archetypal imagery with the unblinking eyes and steady hand of the artist who is wild with the grief and bitter laughter of the son who has forbidden knowledge of his mother and is driven by a mania not to leave a shred of her unexposed, then you have the greatest women of all—Jocasta, Lady Macbeth, Mona Lisa, Grainger, Madame Girard.

Descending further into the hell that is *Dream Palace,* we come to the soul of the story. Dame Edith Sitwell said, "There is no evocation of love more heartrending than the one that Fenton feels for his little brother." It is the love as Euripides and Sophocles understood it. And as it unfolds in all its tenderness and despair, burdened with duty and shame, we moan as the Greek chorus for we know it is doomed. Fenton looks at the sickly little boy who misses his mother so much and knows he cannot carry him further. "Why is it," he asks, "One is even weaker than the other?" A new life was beginning for him. Claire would rather perish in this rat hole than be bought by the mansion and watch the prostitution of his brother. Fenton's anguish grows to the breaking point. He knows that as long as there is Claire, part of his old life is with him, and he wants to destroy that and begin all over again. He feels an urge of violence against this "puny, defiant, impossible little brother." At the same time he has more tenderness for him than for another being. Torn between love and the wish to be free he is overcome with the melancholy, savage irritability and callousness that Hamlet showed when he could not bring himself to act. James Purdy understands with "all the fires of the heart and the crystallizing powers of the brain" (Dame Edith Sitwell) that love and freedom are tragically at odds. Whichever we choose to cut off, we will be left mutilated. There is no comfort for such sorrow.

The scene is now set for the final descent. Fall from grace does not come however directly from the hand of the Queen of Hell, though walking in her husband's shoes makes it inevitable. Circe appears in the form of a beautiful young man, and trancelike, as if he had a foreknowledge of his fate, he follows him into the Halls of Hades. The description of this journey is so controlled that it gives us the hallucinatory feeling of having been there and the terror of it makes us weep.

Then the morning after: "And this morning for Fenton was one that shattered everything he had known." He looks at the cold Claire and sees, ". . . the neck broken softly like a small bird's, the hair around his neck like ruffled feathers." Fenton flees in horror. But he must come back to the scene of his crime. Though the crime was committed while drunk and drugged, and therefore not conscious, he must come back and face his deed. For if he does not return, he is doomed to be a shade in hell, "wandering and groping about without aim."

Why did he kill Claire? Was it indeed because he could no longer be his brother's keeper? Was it an act of mercy to spare him a slow death, was it because he could no longer face his brother in his degradation, or because it was the natural climax after a cannibalistic orgy? It was all that and more.

A work of art is a many faceted gem. Each reader must hold it in his hand and find individual reflection and meaning. The possible interpretations are many: anthropological, psychological, existential. They do not annul each other. The wonder of it is that they complement and re-enforce each other.

Claire was a part of Fenton, the part that died the night of the orgy. Though Fenton and Claire are treated as two, they are two parts of a single epic hero, and in their unity lies the essential unity of the book. Killing Claire then was killing part of himself, the deepest most buried part of his personality and psyche. Castration. It is this that makes us feel we have witnessed a historic, irrevocable act, an act of the epic proportions of Oedipus Rex gouging out his eyes with his mother's brooch.

It is significant that Fenton's downfall and violent aftermath started with the wearing of another man's clothes.* Was his guilt a form of transvestitism, trying to be what he was not, or was it the guilt of taking the husband's place? Hamlet's incestuous sheets. It was both perhaps. Again, one interpretation does not cancel out the other.

The return to the scene of the murder of the being Fenton loved most takes the greatest courage of all, the courage to face the devastating truth within himself against all inner resistance, and the courage to accept the responsibility of his act. It amounts to what in war is called "bravery in the face of the enemy."

* Malcolm's decline came with wearing the clothes given him by his wife Melba, and Amos Ratcliffe's (*Eustace Chisholm and The Works*) spiritual death came with his acceptance of Reuben Masterson's clothes.

The deathwatch and burial of his brother is lyric prose. There is not a word or gesture that is superfluous. It resounds in our ears with the immediacy of the heard voice, the voice of unpretentious truth. Fenton remembers a chest in the attic. It is not a fragrant cedar chest as he hoped it would be, but an old box with broken hinges and a soiled gauzy wedding veil inside. It is not a fit resting place, but it would have to do. And yet, the box with the gauzy veil suggests the womb. What more fitting resting place is there for the little brother who could not live without his mother? Before Fenton can bring himself to carry his brother to his final resting place, he sits down beside him crushed with grief. He knows that once he puts him into the chest he is really dead forever. Then he makes himself do the most undoable of all. He kisses the dead stained lips that he had stopped. It is an agonizing moment, a moment that warns us not "to call any earthly creature blessed" (*Oedipus Rex*).

The ending leaves us lacerated and yet exalted. It is an affirmation of life. Fenton lifts his brother in his arms and carries him *up* the stairs. An ascension. A rebirth. The birth of the existential hero who has made the choice to will his life. He was born into a situation not of his making. Society and the womb formed a crushing combination. To free himself from this vise, desperate steps were necessary. He descended into black hell, courting madness to gain insight otherwise unattainable. To re-emerge liberated means for Fenton Riddleway cutting his tie to the womb and society. This is alienation. Permanent exile. It is the price he pays, and he pays it with dignity. Kissing the stained dead mouth is kissing the root of his sorrow, his mutilation. It is an action fired by a passion for life so intense only those who have known death can have it. It is the dignity of Oedipus as he faces his exile with hollow eyesockets.

James Purdy leads us through a dark world, a world lit up by his insight. The soul of action is completely at one with the meaning of it. Their integration is so perfect that it has the finality of a historic act never to be undone. He makes each word live with his personal breath of life. That's why when Fenton Riddleway utters the most terrible Anglo-Saxon blasphemy at Claire's burial, he restores it to its original meaning and the word sums up our essential tragic human condition. He has us identifying in our very bowels with all his characters — victim and tyrant, corrupters and corrupted. We are everyone and everything from the beginning of time.

Who then is Fenton Riddleway? He is the castaway in the American tradition of Melville and Mark Twain — the passive, impassive victim of circumstance, without skill or knowledge. He is the stranger, but not the stranger of Camus and Sartre. For none of Purdy's characters are abstractions, symbolic of something else. They are *themselves*. Fenton Riddleway is himself with every fiber of his being, with every breath he takes and every word he says. And being truly himself he transcends and becomes us. That is finally his hold on our imagination.

IT'S IN THE NAME: "Don't Call Me By My Right Name" and "LEAVE ME Madame Girard" (Chapter in *Malcolm*)

"Her name was Mrs. Klein. There was something in the meaning that irritated her," so begins James Purdy's outrageous story, "Don't Call Me By My Right Name," about Mrs. Klein née Lois McBane who could not accept her married name. "Names do make a great difference and after six months of marriage she found herself still not liking her name. . . . Lois Klein, she often thought as she lay next to her husband in bed. It is not the name of a woman like myself. It does not reflect my character."

In *Malcolm*, on the other hand, Madame Girard is asked to

surrender her married name and this regal woman who a day before had declared with the self-assurance of a goddess, "You are all dependent on me for life," sinks to her knees before her husband, and kissing his shoes she cries, "My name! You cannot take it. Take the money, the victory, but leave me as I was: Madame Girard."

The passion with which these women fight is so intense that we get the feeling of being present at a historic moment, a transfer of power, Marie Antoinette pleading for her life in the shadow of the guillotine.

That women get married and divorced and that names change in the process is so commonplace and well known that we can hardly understand this desperation without digging into our past and calling on mythology for help. (It is not necessary to know the whys and wherefores to feel the impact of a story, but it deepens our appreciation if we are able to interpret the symbolism and recognize the same primordial notes as resound in myths.)

What's in a name? The feeling has always been that the name of a person or thing is intimately connected with its very nature. To the Babylonians and Egyptians, the name was the essence of the person to whom it was attached. In many primitive and ancient tongues, the word for name and breath or soul is the same. The primitive was aware that he used his breath to form a name. Iago understood the meaning of a name to its deepest stratum when he called it "the immediate jewel of the soul."

If one existed because of one's name, it was also true that one could be wiped out by having one's name eradicated. The American Indian believed that whatever happened to his name happened to him, and he therefore refused to *give* his name to a stranger.

". . . he that filches from me my good name . . . makes me poor indeed," Iago said and, manipulator that he was, used this insight to destroy Desdamona by casting suspicion on her name. With the loss of name, one's identity, the very essence of one's being is destroyed.

James Purdy, his ear so close to the heartbeat of humanity, understands this *essence of being*, and gives us Lois McBane and Madame Girard who fight like the Furies to hold on to the "immediate jewel of the soul."

At one point in "Don't Call Me By My Right Name," Lois declares, "We can't be married, Frank, with that name between us." And Frank exasperated by this feminine logic cries, "Why do you torture me?" With this question he echoes and re-echoes the questions husbands have always asked in various forms: "Why do you nag? Aren't you ever satisfied? What do you want?" Even Freud confessed that after thirty years of studying woman, he still did not know what she wanted. "*Was will das Weib?*" Where husbands and Freud are in the dark, perhaps the poet can shed light.

What does Lois McBane want? The title of the story tells what she does not want. Does this imply she wants to be called by a wrong name? Lois McBane, *her own special name*, can hardly be called wrong. The opposite of *right* is also *left*. Everywhere from time immemorial, the *left* side was favored by females, the *right* by males. While Rhea was bearing Zeus, the story goes, she pressed her fingers into the soil to ease her pangs and up sprang the Dactyls, five females from the *left* hand and five males from her *right*. In palmistry, the *left* hand is the dreamer — the subjective side, the *right* hand is the doer — the objective side. "Right and left have in many languages the dual meaning of the body image on one hand, and moral values on the other. Right also means 'just, correct,' and Left means 'sinister'. . . . Justice and correctness and the rational stand for the Father; the sinister left is the world of the unconscious and pre-rational — a world in which we are still at one with Mother." (Karl Stern, *The Flight From Woman*)

Lois' *right* name came to her through a legal contract, man-made, rational. It indeed does not reflect her character which was formed long before marriage, nor can it tell us anything of her roots and heritage. All it reveals is that she is the wife of Mr. Klein. That this has robbed her of the immediate jewel of her soul and turned her into her husband's property is expressed by Frank when he says arrogantly, "No wife of mine would ever be old or fat." Would he trade her in for newer model if she got old and fat? Lois can accept none of this — neither does she intend to fulfill her contract in any way, "I don't want to have babies, Frank. . . . Categorically not." However, she does want Frank and she wants marriage without that name between them. She wants the original matrimony — as the etymology of the word implies, a rule by mothers. A woman did not surrender her name when she made the rules, inheritance was matrilineal. When marriage, as in patriarchal society, means separation from the mother and her name, it is felt as an abduction and rape — as the custom of carrying the bride over the threshold reminds us. In wanting her *left* name, her maiden name, Lois wants *the world in which we are still at one with mother*. That this matrix and the sheltered girlhood days that come with it are what woman yearns for is expressed in some other stories by James Purdy.

In "A Good Woman," Maud ". . . always remembered her mother with pleasure instead of grief." In "Cracks," Nera says, "My mother has been dead many, many years . . . . Yet she is the only comfort I still have. Only my mother loved me. Nobody ever loved me but her . . . ." In "You Reach For Your Hat," Jennie tells how her husband never noticed her charms and says wistfully, "My mother knew I was beautiful." And Madame Girard, always articulating her unconscious in poetic picture language, expresses it this way, "The trap opened and closed . . . and all the old and dear things were replaced by marriage."

Frank, in "Don't Call Me By My Right Name," with the blindness and self-righteous indignation of those living on the right side sees none of this. What he sees is that his wife is having an *insane whim* while drunk. Her nagging, her *holding up his name to ridicule*, has nearly driven him out of his mind, and not being able to make her listen to reason he resorts to violence, beating her to the ground. From this floor position, which surprised neither of them enough to interrupt their flow of words, she tells the world, "I can't decide if I can go on with his name . . . I know . . . what the sensible decision is, and tomorrow, of course, when I'm sober I will wish I had taken it." Sober, she will do what every sensible person does, conform to the right side of life and deny what the left-sided heartbeat tells her. But that sinister left side won't be denied. As Jung puts it in *Modern Man in Search of a Soul*, man's "reason has done violence to natural forces which seek their revenge and only await the moment when the partition falls to overwhelm the conscious life with destruction." We meet most of Purdy's characters at the very moment when the partition is falling and the natural forces are wreaking destruction with a vengeance.

Later, lying bleeding on the sidewalk where Frank knocked her down because "she didn't want to be Mrs. Klein," Lois screams, "There is something wrong with my head. My God . . . . I'm in awful pain." What she would not surrender willingly has been taken by force. Rape. Violated to the core of her being, her maidenhead is bleeding. She resorts then to woman's last two weapons — tongue and handbag. Still on the ground she attacks Frank Klein with both. "Call me a cab, you cheap son of a bitch," she commands from her low station and knocks him against the wall with her purse where he stands in surprise, not comprehending at all that

17

the anger of eons of surrender was in that thrust. In this one image, James Purdy condensed the bitter war between the sexes — universal, eternal, and unresolved.

If Lois McBane could not surrender her *left* name, Madame Girard could not give up her *right* name. Between these two polarities lie thousands of years of human history, encompassing the transition from matriarchy to patriarchy. In ancient Egypt and other places, rule was matrilineal and man could only be pharaoh by marrying the queen. Once woman finally realized that she had been conquered and the power had gone from her maiden name the way of her maidenhood, she did the next best thing: rule with the name of her husband. His name became her scepter, her phallus. As this had to be done behind the throne or underground it had a daemonic, devious quality. After Kore, which means *maiden,* was abducted and became Queen of Hades, her name changed to Persephone, *destructive one.**

The chapter in *Malcolm* titled *"Leave me* Madame Girard" reveals more in a handful of pages about woman's place in the scheme of things than the millions of conscious and self-conscious words written of late about the second sex.

The day Madame Girard received her proposal of marriage has the pastoral setting of Kore among the flowers of the Eleusinian meadow. At first she refused, "of course," and then:

> Another few days had passed, and Fall shaking down the last leaves, he asked her again. This time, silently weeping over her passing youth, she could not speak but nodded rather vigorously for a woman of her temperament. Girard Girard, like the magician he was, already holding the ring in the palm of his hand pushed it with

* In *As You Like It,* Shakespeare expresses this transformation as, "A Maid is May when she's a maid, but the sky changes when she's a wife."

painful vigor onto her finger, and kissed her heavily on the mouth. . . . "You are then victorious," Madame Girard had said.

This act of putting the ring on her finger, taking place at every wedding, is transformed by the poet to its original meaning — conquest, rape. We are witnessing the enactment of a rite that has its roots in archetypal experience. There is a profound silence in the congregation at this point of the ceremony, and the words, "With this ring I thee wed," stir us anew, no matter how often we have heard them.

Madame Girard's words at the end of the rite, "You are then victorious," express how differently this sexual encounter is experienced by man and woman. As Erich Neumann states in *Amor & Psyche*, "What for the masculine is aggression, victory, rape and the satisfaction of desire . . . is for the feminine destiny, transformation, and the profoundest mystery of life."

This experience is further expressed by Madame Girard, "The trap opened and closed . . . and all old and dear things were forever replaced by marriage." The same earth trap opened and closed for the maiden Kore and took her from her flowers and the bosom of Demeter. And just as in the Greek myth, with the deflowering of Kore, nature itself was deflowered and the sky changed from May to November, Madame Girard's landscape is transformed, ". . . frightened at the changes that suddenly appeared about her on all sides, like the cracks in an ice floe . . . . Looking past him to where the trees stood nearly naked over the lagoon, she said, 'I will now be Madame Girard to the entire world. I will be no one else.'"

It is a historic moment, the crowning of a queen who reluctantly and not without rebellion has given up the carefree spring days of the princess, and now accepts her destiny and strange identity. The princess is dead. Long live the queen!

19

But let her not forget the emblem in her crown is her husband's.

And now that she is Madame Girard and no one else, comes the coup de grace. "You are no longer Madame Girard . . . You have ceased to exist . . . You are now — history," Girard Girard proclaims.

What led to this catastrophic moment? "She had never loved Girard, and Girard, of course, had never precisely loved her as a woman. He had worshipped her, satisfying his appetite with the blossoming bodies of common women, but . . . his worship had grown with the years . . . he had never ceased keeping a whole altar of lights burning for her. Now suddenly . . . he would no longer light candles to her. The last match had been put to the last wick. . . . Girard Girard no longer loved Madame Girard."

There is such an immediacy in the poetry of Madame Girard's thoughts, that it becomes a moment of greatest importance to all of us. With Girard Girard no longer loving Madame Girard, love for woman has left the world.

Primeval woman had no love for her husband. He was a stranger and no primitive could accept a stranger. She could only love her flesh and blood: Her mother and her children. When she reigned and enacted her wishes, she consummated her love for her sons. She was the physically loved mother, Mater Natura. With her dethronement, her nature was violated by man-made incest taboo. This change from matriarchal rule to patriarchal one is expressed with the greatest immediacy by Aeschylus in *The Oresteia*, where the Erinys, the avenger of violated Mother cries,

> O, new gods, ye overrun old law, ancient justice
> Ye tear them, in overturning them from my hand
> And I, covered with shame, righteously indignant
> In vengeance I seed the soil with poison
> That dripped from my heart.

To placate the Erinys for the violation of nature, Athene promises,

> In an honorable dwelling
> Near the temple of Erechteus, thou wilt in future
> Be highly honored of men and women
> As no other country honored thee.*

In this honorable dwelling, Girard Girard lit a whole altar of lights. *She was not loved precisely as a woman,* but as a sainted mother. Mater Spiritualis. Woman is now split in two. The other side of the Madonna is the whore with whom Girard Girard satisfied his sexual appetites. If Madame Girard becomes the enshrined Virgin Mother, Malcolm becomes Christ, her divine son. Only unconsummated love can take this spiritual form — it is troubadour love, the love Dante felt for Beatrice. And now she has been thrown from her pedestal. *Mother* the word not long ago spoken with reverence is now a word of contempt. She is known as the monster in the nursery, castrator and devourer of sons. There is no love — physical or spiritual — left for her. In vain she cries, "I am Madame Girard . . . . The whole world has always known me as she, the whole world will not so quickly lose its memory." And to this Girard Girard answers cynically, "The world remembers only what power and money tell it."

"O new gods, ye overrun old law." The new gods according to Girard Girard are Money and Power, and with them woman and marriage have depreciated. What is a name in this new order of things if it can be taken from the wife and given to a whore? Madame Girard cries, "You mean to destroy my identity then?" And Girard answers à la Simone de Beauvoir, "You are completely free, don't you see?" What kind of existentialism is this that frees Madame Girard from being Madame Girard? Nothing in her biography and biology

---

* As quoted in *Mothers and Amazons* by Helen Diner, ed. and trans. by John Philip Lundin. Page 37.

21

has prepared her for this liberation from her name. Who is she now deprived of her name and the duties that came with it? When she was originally robbed of her *left* name she was degraded to the second sex, and now deprived of her *right* name, will she become the third sex? Is this the loveless, faceless creature who dons wig and falsies and can only masquerade as woman? And while she is this nameless shade in limbo, her ears are assaulted by noise from all directions. The advocates of the third sex tell her the world is her oyster. She can be anything she wants to be, without giving up anything, and above all, she must never be satisfied with what she is or has. The high priests of the new gods — the advertisers — thunder at her that to fulfill herself means to fill herself full with the things that money can buy. The name of her new role is *Consumer* and her identification is the computor number on her charge-a-plate.

Madame Girard who a little while ago was an indispensable life force, "Without me, your life would have no imagination . . . . my spirit and will are all that keep you going. You are all of you dependent on me for life," knowing what is in store for her as a nameless woman thrown out of her honorable dwelling, falls to her knees and kisses Girard Girard's beautifully shined shoes — the symbol of his male power and money, "Leave me with what I was. Leave me Madame Girard." Well might she moan with the Erinys of Aeschylus, "Woe, that I must suffer this." Again man's reason has done violence to natural forces which must seek revenge. Will a second car, third TV set and monthly alimony placate the Erinys this time?

It is a nightmare — and just as a nightmare expresses a warning to the dreamer of his psychic disturbance, so the visionary poet — the universal dreamer that he is — sends out warnings of the psychic disturbance of his epoch. It is for the rest of us to act and react.

What's in a name? This may well be the crucial question of

22

our generation. Is it in the words of Girard Girard "what money and power tell it," reducible to a perforated number, or is it in the words of Shakespeare, "the immediate jewel of the soul"? On whichever way we choose to regard it depends the fate of mankind.

THE FORSAKEN: *Malcolm*

Texas Quarterly, Spring, 1967

In "Sermon" the speaker declares, "You have nothing with which to win." This is true for most of James Purdy's characters, as they stumble dazed into a world where they never find footing. It is a harsh, indifferent world that offers no protection to the weak and ignores the helpless in their death throes. "It has all been a mistake your coming here," says the speaker. Malcolm, the defenseless child hero of Purdy's picaresque novel *Malcolm,* has no weapon to fight the overwhelming odds against him. The destiny of such a "mistake" is forecast by the speaker:

> "You are bad off and getting more so, and sadly enough when you get in the worst shape of all so that you think you will not be able to go on for another second, the road ahead is still worse yet. . . ."

No use fleeing from these words of horror and despair, for the speaker is an extension of the voice within. He reminds us, "I'm the possessor of your ears." And so too is the storyteller who speaks to our soul with the first magic sentence of this tale.

"In front of one of the most palatial hotels in the world," the story begins, "a very young man was accustomed to sit on a bench which, when the light fell in a certain way, shone like gold." The artist and storyteller instinctively evokes this aura of enchantment when he is dealing with the origin of things — genesis — and with an event as timeless and ever recurring as sunrise.

Malcolm has a waiting look of obviously expecting some-body. Throughout the saga the boy is waiting for his father, though the whereabouts of his mother is never mentioned. In mythology the mother *is* and *is not*. She is the earth from which the hero sprang, the basket in which he is discovered, the golden egg, the ocean foam or dolphin on which he comes riding in. She is every woman he meets on the way. If *she is not* a specific person, and if no father is present, the feeling is evoked of the purest type of orphan whose birth is wel-comed and celebrated by no one. Such an orphan is Malcolm.

Malcolm is surrounded by the womb; it is the golden bench, the ocean nearby — primal waters from which came all life — and it is the seashells in his room which he puts to his ear and listens to the rhythm of the tides by, moon rhythm, rhythm of the womb.

The money that paid for Malcolm's physical needs is run-ning out and the golden bench has become a *useless ornament*, as useless as the eggshell is to the newly hatched chick. It is at this moment, when the womb can no longer sustain him, that the boy needs his father's support. If mother is the nat-ural world, father is the existential world, the world of thought, of law and order, of adventure, travel, and tasks to be done — civilization. It is in this world he must continue his growth into fully human maturity.

Malcolm, who is fourteen, is at the age when in a primitive culture he would have undergone puberty rites, as transition into manhood there was not left to chance. The tribal boy was removed from his mother, given instructions by his male eld-ers, and made to *experience a spiritual rebirth* through the father — an existential birth. Without guidance and strength from his father the son cannot realize and fulfill himself. With-out this help his is a misbegotten birth and the boy is crippled. It is at this most crucial moment of his life that Malcolm finds himself abandoned and comes to the attention of his self-appointed initiator, the astrologer Mr. Cox.

Mr. Cox feels disturbed at the sight of Malcolm.

> . . . and he felt obscurely that the young man on the
> bench offered a comment, even a threat, certainly a criti-
> cism of his own career and thought — not to say existence.

Mr. Cox too, who is fifty and looks more like seventy or eighty,
was once an innocent, helpless, and bewildered boy. He sees
Malcolm as a projection of that child. But this unexpected re-
minder may lead to compassion, and that will never do for a
man who has made it his career to exploit weakness. He must,
therefore, destroy the child in order to go on without conflict
in his pretentious, destructive life.

Before Mr. Cox can take Malcolm into his power, he has to
find out if he belongs to anyone. Malcolm tells Mr. Cox of his
missing father. Throughout the narration we never know for
certain if there is a father or if he is a figment of the boy's
imagination. And since the story is completely enacted without the author's ever intruding his own explanations, we
never find out. We are thrown into the same twilight state of
consciousness that Malcolm inhabits, where the border between dream and reality is obscured. There is, however, indi-
cation that he never had a father, for his references to him
hint more at ignorance than at knowledge. Someone who had
a father, even for a short time, would not be quite as lost and
vulnerable as Malcolm. He would not so quickly accept "help"
from the first man who comes along, for he would have been
warned not to talk to strangers. It is obvious that no one
has warned and prepared Malcolm for anything.

Malcolm tells of travels with his father, of fine restaurants,
horseback riding, sailing, ". . . and sitting in big hotel rooms
with him looking at me so proud and happy. He was glad I was
just the way I was, and I was glad he was just the way he
was . . . ."

This recitation expresses all the yearning of the abandoned
child who cannot bear the pain of his rejection and dreams of

a father who shares the adventure of life. It expresses mankind's deep longing for a caring and protecting father who accepts us as we are. It also expresses a wish for a father of whom the son can be proud — a father who accepts the responsibility for his "mistake," the accident that spawned new life.

Malcolm does not know his birthday. The astrologer is put out at first, as he needs this information to cast the boy's horoscope. But now he realizes it is irrelevant under what sign Malcolm was born; someone so abandoned as to have no one to remind him of his birthday has no lucky star — no favorable day to start a trip. And being the *spirit of a depleted epoch*, this initiator believes that it is not important who or what you are becoming, but whom you know. He gives, therefore, his foundling apprentice a commencement gift — the first street address.

Thus Malcolm leaves the bench and begins his travels, not towards life and self-realization in the company of the good father, but under the misguidance of Mephistopheles towards destruction and death.

Significantly enough, the first address takes him to the black undertaker Estel Blanc. This chapter, seen as through a glass darkly, is sustained by the Purdian humor that makes us accept the most terrifying visions and absurd situations as a matter of course. The humor is that of someone who has never lost his astonishment at the strange antics and outrageous behavior of man. It gets directly to the core of things and leaves us helplessly naked. All we can do is laugh at the ridiculous sight.

There is something of the mystery of the Mass in the scene in which they sip Spanish chocolate under a cathedral-high ceiling — in the toast they eat, in the incense-laden air, and in the sudden appearance of an elusive figure called Cora Naldi.

> Malcolm was never able to tell anybody later what or
> who Cora Naldi was. He was not even sure at times she

was a woman, for she had a very deep voice and he could never tell whether her hair was white or merely platinum or whether she was colored like Estel or white like himself. She both sang and danced in loose shawls, and gave a kind of recitatif when her throat got tired from her singing numbers.

It is a foreboding vision, a vision of how the first severance from the womb is experienced, and can be formulated only in the vocabulary of the psyche — pictures that float past and vanish. It leaves Malcolm with an inexplicable unease that gives him the desperate need for a father's hand to save him from drowning. Malcolm has started on his road to death while at the other end Circe is dancing in *loose shawls*, luring him back into the primal waters.

Yes, there could be no doubt, he was beginning life, and with his usual silent evening prayer addressed to his father, wherever he might be, dead or alive, lost or found, he hastened back to his hotel suite.

The second address leads Malcolm into the home of Kermit and Laureen Raphaelson, where he falls right into the middle of a sordid marital wrestling bout. They invite the boy to join in by making him referee, and unashamed, they consummate the brawl with a sexual embrace. "You'll understand when you are married . . . ." Laureen promises the boy, who has become drowsy by the complexities of wedded bliss.

Malcolm's *elegant and untouched appearance* remains unblemished and unsullied by his step into morass. His impervious innocence is his strength and weakness. It makes him immune to corruption but leaves him utterly unprotected from the destructive forces descending on him. He sums up his first exposure to marriage: "Married love is the strangest thing of all." When marriage is seen through the eyes of a child, not yet blurred by the propaganda of the institution, who can disagree?

Kermit is a midget and Laureen has *propensities for street-walking*. "The contrast between the two was stupefying to him . . . Kermit so small, Laureen so large and plump and commanding."

The women Malcolm meets are so powerful that they dwarf their husbands. To the fatherless child they are as voracious and incestuous as in the ancient matriarchy.*

Kermit, the beautiful midget with his fifteen cats, his hammer and paintbrush, is as demoniacal as any gnome or mythical blacksmith in a mountain cave, drawing energy from a smoldering inner fire. And any inquiry whether he is dwarf or midget makes him stamp his foot and turn red with rage. "I am not big . . . but I am no different from other men — fundamentally."

Mr. Cox explains to the bewildered Malcolm who is too simple to understand why anyone should be upset by *what* he is:

> "His mother evidently never told him he was one, and never referred to it, so that when finally he grew up — well, he didn't actually know it. The day will come when he will have to admit he is a midget, and go on from there."

This most shattering moment comes when Laureen abandons Kermit. "I was only her pre-husband . . . her break-in man. Now she has gone on to the real equipment."

A midget, in the dream language of the book, is someone who is not equipped to satisfy voluptuous Venus. It is the impotent rage of Cupid, with his little bow and arrow, who is teased and flirted with by his mother, only to be forsaken outside her bedroom door when Mars takes over with the *real equipment*. At this moment when "I have just given up

* In some drawings, Isis is full bodied and statuesque, and Osiris is a miniature man, barely reaching his wife's hips. On some ancient Minoan cameos and rings the Great Mother is portrayed with a dwarflike creature beside her, who is son and husband at the same time. Rhea, the Greek Mother Goddess, is shown with dactyls, minute phalli, without a man attached to them as yet.

my entire world by admitting who I really am . . . ," Kermit can't endure to hear Malcolm magnifying his father's name one more time, and he says the unsayable, "Shit on your father."

Why glorify a deserter? A true father would not have deserted the conjugal bed, leaving mother and son free to act out their fantasies. He would have taken his son from the seducing mother and shown him how to grow into manly size.

If Kermit now has to learn to live with the terrible knowledge of his sexual mutilation, Malcolm must learn to live without the faith in his father. But Malcolm is utterly crushed by Kermit's blasphemy. Kermit then reconciles him, "Don't I know that your father was a princely type, judging by the son. . . ."

Royalty or not, this father is a deserter — and we cannot quarrel with the blasphemy coming from another crippled victim of desertion. No one comprehends the full meaning of abandonment better than the son who knows he has no father to wait for. He experiences the terror of primal loneliness and solitude, for he is exposed to all the elements and beasts of prey.

Kermit is uniquely himself and at the same time symbolically a part of Malcolm — his sex, his phallus. Kermit cries, "You have no right to desert me. . . . I'm dependent on you so, I have nobody else to depend on." No one has given Malcolm the strength and shown him how to carry this *impossible little man.* Malcolm feels he cannot accept his invitation to a new home without Kermit. "I *want* to come. . . . But I'm afraid I can't." An unconscious reason holds him back. This reason is symbolized in the stunted form of Kermit. It is the realization of Oedipus that to him all mansions belong to Jocasta — off limits — and that he is condemned therefore to a life of exile. This crushing knowledge is expressed in this most despairing paragraph, when Kermit, the Kermit part of Malcolm,

29

cannot open the door to the Girards, who have come to fetch him to their summer estate:

> He knew now that he could never go with them. He was too used to poverty, to the routine of deprivation, to his little empty life of complaint and irritations, and the final inanity when he tucked himself in his small bed. To be suddenly translated into a car with a monogram that looked like a vehicle from another civilization, to be surrounded by what was, in effect, royalty, and to see Malcolm enthroned as a favorite — he could never do this. He retreated still further back, and as he did so, the movement of his back pushed open the door, and all the cats seeing their prison opened, rushed out with cries of wildness and relief into the front room and began scratching and meowing on the pane of the tall glass door before which Madame Girard now stood.

The cats in the back room which he locked up when he married Laureen are Kermit's animal instincts. He had suppressed them, and now that he faces his mutilation and the subsequent limitation to his life, his instincts are freed and take control of the scene. They prevent him from opening the front door. The abandoned boy, wounded by every contact with a world that has no love for him, can only rely on what nature gave him — his instincts.

The most despairing line of the book and perhaps in all of James Purdy's work is Mr. Cox's prognostication of Kermit's doom, "Kermit will never be able to say yes again to anything." It is final and inevitable. It is the fate of all children who being deserted by their father are robbed of the birthright to reach mature growth.

The third address takes Malcolm to the chateau of Madame and Mr. Girard where the ceilings are as high as at the funeral palace of Estel Blanc. Someone else's home is strange territory — unpredictable, not to be entered without armor. To the child who has *nothing with which to win* it is another potential funeral chapel — the gingerbread house of Hansel and Gretel.

Madame Girard is queen in her domain, attended by beautiful young courtiers and princes. She is wrathfully jealous of devotion given anyone else and must destroy Malcolm's longing for his father.

> "I do not think your father exists. . . . I have *never* thought he did. . . . And what is more . . . *nobody* thinks he exists, or ever did exist."

In the matriarchy there is room for but one despot — Madame Girard. The longing for a father threatens her rule, for it asserts that she cannot fill *all* needs. Mounting discontent could lead to rebellion and to her dethronement. She must protect herself. With no father to intervene she is free to castrate the beautiful "sons," that surround her, and render them powerless.*

Mr. Girard is a magnate, maker of presidents and man of the hour, and he must have Malcolm in the bargain. "I seem to see it (life) starting all over again in you." In a custody fight over the boy with Madame Girard, he spirits Malcolm away from the familiar, to the horticultural gardens in a strange part of town. In the greenhouse devoted to tropical plants he urges his would-be son to *choose* him.

> "Madame Girard shall not have you to herself. . . . Come live with me and my new wife, accept all we have to offer, feel secure and loved with us. . . ."

No sooner has Malcolm agreed, in his desperate need for a home, than Girard deserts him, not on a magic golden bench this time but on a chair made of stone, as cold and dead as a grave marker. And indeed the desertion turns this paradisical setting into a cemetery.

---

* The priests who served Isis and other Great Mothers were castrated and wore female garb in her honor.

"Please do not go away without me. . . . Take me with you."

"Quite out of the question," Mr. Girard told him, "My engagement is of the utmost importance, and you would only be in the way. . . ."

Mr. Girard forgets to return. Out of sight out of mind. To a father to whom only what money can buy is real, a son has no reality. Mr. Girard is not even aware of his criminal act of abandonment. It was mostly a matter of winning a contest with Madame Girard, and now that he has won he can forget the object of the contest and devote himself to his new wife.

Preliterate man, in the initiation rites, led his son through a symbolic womb — a cave, dense foliage, or a shelter like the greenhouse. Had this tribal father been distracted by other pressing matters in the midst of this acting out of the second birth, there would have resulted a strangulation, a still birth.

. . . he (Malcolm) heard from behind the closing of the tall gates of the horticultural gardens, and the snap as they locked themselves against him.

It is the snap of the guillotine.

From the gates of Gethsemane, the forsaken son is whisked towards Golgotha on a motorcycle driven by Gus, a Negro youth. And without benefit of the astrologer Malcolm meets a star. Melba, *Number 1 chanteuse* in the world of the *contemporaries*, finds herself between husbands, and when she sees Malcolm she promptly decides to make him her *Number 3*. For Malcolm it is the only solution.

Too young for the army, too unprepared to continue his schooling and become a scientist, too untrained for ordinary work — what was left for him but marriage?

The fatherless boy, who has never been taught to be a man, is fit only for a matriarchal marriage. He must accept the second-sex role of being kept, of being a sexual plaything on

32

command, without any human rights of his own. "What did I buy you for, kiddy?" complains Melba when Malcolm's vigor flags.

> Having lost Girard and Mr. Cox, Kermit and the bench, he held more tightly to Melba than he had ever held to any other human being. . . .

Melba, the jet-age queen, does not let a little matter like Malcolm's extreme youth stand in her way. "Mature him up," she orders her ex-husband Gus, "Old Number 1." She promises Malcolm, "He'll be like a father to you."

To Gus, instant maturity is achieved in a house of ill repute. Malcolm, with nothing but his instincts to guide him, knows better. "But one or two tattoos for a wedding is surely . . . well usual," he says, wondering *where he had ever heard what he had just said.*

His psyche prompts him. It expresses the great inner need for a ritual that draws the dividing line between childhood and maturity. To withstand the pain, while a brave totem animal is being tattooed on his chest, satisfies the profound need to identify and be at one with the father. Malcolm's amazing bravery, which *the tattoo artist had never quite encountered before*, would have filled a preliterate father with pride. But Gus passes out at the sight of blood and dies not long afterwards. Without the *father* this initiation attempt miscarries too.

> For the first time since his father's disappearance, Malcolm shed not just a few, but a torrent of tears . . . and at times he whimpered like a five-year-old child.

Malcolm has one more encounter with *father*. After his tenth or twelfth rum sour, his usual fare with Melba, he sees his *father* and follows him into the lavatory of the night club. But the *middle-aged unemphatically distinguished man* does not recognize his *son*. "If you will not allow me to recognize you, let me show you your own identification mark . . . ," says Malcolm. But *father* becomes alarmed at this attempt at physical contact and knocks the boy to the marble floor, where he sustains a head wound. "Arrest that pederast," *father* tells the police. In a society where fatherhood and its responsibilities are not accepted and understood, a boy's desperate need for the paternal touch is declared *pederasty.**

Melba advises her young husband, who is bleeding to death, "With my fame and money and your special gift, blow your father." When a man's inner needs are not recognized, a materialistic trinity takes over: fame, money, sex.

"Maybe my father never existed," Malcolm said and his tones were now like those of Melba's.

The faith and longing that sustained Malcolm are now dead. Malcolm faces the moral catastrophe of our times, that which arises when archetypes are attacked and old values lose their validity without new, satisfying ones coming to replace them. Melba's way of filling this void is a modern slogan, "Drink more and have more frequent conjugal duties." No one having given Malcolm any other guidance or values, he can only accept Melba's. And so the *short long life* of Malcolm is ended by *acute alcoholism and sexual hyperaesthesia* — the disease that attacks the body when the spirit has been starved to death.

In *Malcolm*, James Purdy tells us the eternal story of the child in the vocabulary of our time. It will have to be told again and again to remind us of our childhood, and of the eternal bewildered child within us that needs the love and care and guidance toward self-realization that no one gave Malcolm.

* In patriarchal Rome, a father recognized his son publicly by placing him on his knee. The knee, *genu* in Latin, was thought to be the seat of man's generative powers.

AUNT ALMA: *The Nephew*

The *University of Windsor Review*, Fall, 1967
"Man, if indeed thou knowest what thou doest, thou art blessed; but if thou knowest not, thou art cursed, and a transgressor of the law."*

In *The Nephew*, James Purdy unfolds the story of Alma Mason, the Puritan spinster, who through the death of the nephew she loved emerges from the cursed darkness to the blessed light. This painful, tortuous emergence to consciousness, man's Promethian conquest, is told by the author in most moving, poetic language.

The story unfolds tenderly and inevitably, barely perceptible to the naked eye and with it as tenderly and inevitably the heart and soul of Alma Mason. Suddenly it seems, "night lifted from night," and there is the miracle of full bloom in the light of day. This full bloom in Alma is all the more miraculous as it came late, at the threshold of death. If indeed there is meaning to the longevity of life, to Alma those years were granted to gain that high form of consciousness necessary to self-knowledge and self-realization. Before she dies she knows who she is; she is at one with herself.

Alma Mason of Rainbow Center understood and knew nothing of life and people and what was going on around her in her own home town. Her brother Boyd, who lived with her, blamed it on her having been away, teaching fifth grade in a nearby state. To blame the geographical distance of a few miles for her ignorance is laughable, of course. Her awayness was emotional and due to Calvinist pride. It was a pride so great that it would not let her admit to herself that she was weak and fallible. "I don't feel guilty about anything." Pride had built an impenetrable wall around her, shutting her off from the living experience of feeling herself a human being

* Trans. in M. R. James, *The Apocryphal New Testament* (Oxford, 1924), p. 33.

among human beings. This remoteness, accompanied by the anger of the selfrighteous, the irritability of the virtuous, together with the passion for being surrounded always by her own property kept her at such a distance that she could not see anyone or anything.

During the five years that her young nephew, Cliff, had come to live with her and her brother (after his parents were killed in an airplane crash) Alma and Boyd were *away* most of the time, but once Cliff had enlisted in the army they talked of nothing else. They waited impatiently for each paltry, uninformative letter, touchingly quarreling over the meaning of the banal words. When the telegram came that Cliff was missing in Korea: "For Alma, from that moment on, Cliff was more alive than ever, and his homecoming a future actuality which must crown all her hopes and longings." For the first time in her unlived life, she became aware of unfulfilled hopes and the bittersweet pain of longing. The impenetrable wall of her pride was pierced and the arrow found a vulnerable spot in a heart that was human after all.

Now that the letters had stopped coming: "At 9:00 each morning, nonetheless, Alma went to the front door and waited . . . as the postman made his rounds, watching him like this each day brought her to a kind of inventory of who was left and who was dead in her immediate neighborhood . . . ."

Together with a secret humiliation, nibbling away some more of her pride, that she was the only person who received no mail, she became aware of her neighbors' existence and for the first time she thought about them: "Most of the time she thought about people . . . with a growing sense of mystery and unease . . . . She became increasingly dissatisfied with her understanding and knowledge of adult problems and lives. And now with Cliff 'missing' she found herself left only with adult problems . . . her neighbors."

Alma looked at the people around her and parts of herself

stared back. This knowledge, born of love, that we share a nature and rhythm with everything that exists is poignantly expressed in all of James Purdy's work. At this point, however, Alma was not aware of this truth. And there are comical, all-too-human episodes where she sternly demands of her neighbors to correct the very weaknesses she was guilty of. Before she could understand this common humanity she had first to stand trial, be convicted, humbled and chastened to such a degree that she had nothing left to lose.

What she witnessed was the same motif repeating itself all around her. People cursed with not knowing what they were doing, people escaping by various means the confrontation with themselves and because of this destroying themselves and those dependent on their love. And just as in the judicial court ignorance of the law is no excuse, it becomes clear that before the tribunal of life the ignorant transgressor is held responsible and meets terrible punishment, often unto the tenth generation. When tragedy struck her neighbors' homes it was as "simple and terrible and complete" as in the Greek tragedy.

Later when Alma suffered from the transgressions of her own ignorance she said:

> People have tried *not* to hurt me, to keep things from me all my life. . . . But no matter how often or well they hid the truth from me, it always got to me last, and hurt me then a thousand times more than if they had told it to me at the beginning.

She might have added that in just this way she always hid the truth from herself and now it all had caught up with her and the blows hurt a thousand times more on her aged back.

Her retirement and the nephew being away left her with a "sudden engulfing emptiness." She was "uneasily aware now that many of her hours were spent in a dim dream-like reshaping of Cliff's life . . . ." It was then she decided to give

37

this reshaping concreteness, in the form of a written memorial. It did not occur to her that all she knew of him was what the *dim dream-like* appearances told her. Her practical mind, *the part that made the speeches*, told her to write a biography into a record book, like an inventory. For this she needed the formal facts of his life, *what other people saw and knew about him*. In pursuit of this information she was further drawn into the life of her neighbors and the whole town, it seemed, became involved in helping her write the memorial. She needed people now, but being still wary of accepting any help gratis, she invited them to her home and plied them with generous portions of chocolate cream-pie and marble sponge cake baked in the wonderful colonial kitchen she inherited from her mother. She got to feel a little more at home in the place of her birth and learned to enjoy playing the role of the hostess. Having stepped so far from her isolating pride, she left herself wide open to self-knowledge. To her shock she found out that everyone knew more about Cliff than she did. James Purdy expresses this realization in this profoundly moving paragraph:

> In the deepening twilight of her life, she came more and more to the slow, conscious and terribly clear feeling that *they* all knew a great deal more about Cliff . . . than she could ever know. She, who had cared for him more than anybody else; she, to whom Cliff meant not just everything now but perhaps all there had ever been . . . she alone, still waited for his letters. . . . Yet all these people who no longer expected him knew *more* about him than she could ever know.

Had Alma realized that this terrible clear feeling overcomes everyone who has the courage and time to reflect about those they love and that as Boyd told her later, "We none of us, I'm afraid, know anybody or know one another," she might have found some consolation in a shared human failing and sorrow, but now she had to wrestle alone with this terrible clear feeling and question herself where she failed. No longer could she assert, "I don't feel guilty about anything."

With poetic insight the author chose the words, "twilight of her life," for it is only in the twilight of dawn of the child and the twilight of dusk of the aged when boundaries and outlines are obscured that one experiences those *lightning-illumined seconds* that reveal the truth. The busy generation in between that must labor by the sweat of its brow in the noonday sun has no time to see anything. The artist, too, stands apart in the twilight of the periphery and shares in the poetic play of the very young and very old that is eternal and truly wise.

However, a lifetime spent in the escape of self-knowledge did not let her surrender so easily. That dark creature within Alma yearning for the light was also afraid of it, and retracted. And as a result Alma had not overcome her insomnia — the affliction of people who fear their dreams. But dreams will not be denied. If they are not allowed to enter by the front gate in the dark of night, they will enter by sidesluices and overpower one in daylight. Alma met her nightmare in the person of the mad Mrs. Laird who said in her presence, ". . . Alma could never do anything right and so she bossed everybody, telling them how to do things right . . . ." If this were not enough chastening truth to swallow for one day, Mrs. Laird added, "Alma was to all intents and purposes a wife to her own brother. . . ." For the first time straightlaced Alma lost her composure.

In a beautiful example of how the unconscious breaks through and becomes conscious, Alma had an imagined conversation with her neighbor, the old Mrs. Barrington, whose garden was the show-place of the state. At first Alma was in control of the conversation and told Mrs. Barrington what *her mask of good breeding and civility* would in real life have prevented her, ". . . I have never heard you initiate any conversation or terminate one which did not have as its sole subject the pre-eminence of your own things. Your possessions, your land, your this-and-that." *Then quite unexpectedly as it might have done in real life, this imaginary conversation shot beyond the foreknowledge of the imaginer.* Her inner self, that she was unaware of, had Mrs. Barrington say, "Cliff was as much to you in the way of one of your possessions, Alma, as my yard or my garden, or my house or my trumpet vine . . . ."

Being told that she was incestuous, incompetent, and a person who regarded her nephew as a trumpet vine would have made a lesser person turn to the comfort of the hollow walking-cane filled with liquor used by her neighbor Minnie Clyde Hawke. But Alma the Presbyterian sought no crutch or palliative, and she turned to no intermediary before the inner judge. Every day she chose to seat herself before the blank pages of the record book and to face the accusation that she did not know anything of the nephew she loved and that her own life was as blank as her knowledge of Cliff.

Then from the innermost depth emerged the part that she never knew existed within her. *She found a quiet and concentrated something which surprised her.* This quiet concentrated something unfolded and revealed the young Cliff:

> He possessed that astonishing fresh look, as if he had just come out of the forest, perhaps, or even pond, still dripping a little from his bath.

It was the divine child, Balder, Adonis, Eros, Christ — bridegroom and son. She had sheltered this god of love in her home and not recognized him, and now that he was gone she was the mater dolorosa, Virgin Mother, weeping over her sacrificed son. No wonder: *When Cliff left, Alma and Boyd became permanently and very old, their correct age.*

40

*When vigor or hope stirred in them, it was almost always per-
haps because they found themselves talking of him.*

How is it that in the core of this descendant of Calvin lay
buried this pagan idol? Our archaic past cannot be wiped out
by dogma and the more one denies the pagan the more deeply
repressed it is. Alma, the Protestant, protested too much. And
now, to find out who she was, (necessary to one's feeling of
unity), she had to return to the fundamental facts of her own
being by renouncing all authority and tradition that shaped
her conscious life.

Small wonder the pages of the record book remained blank.
Cliff's brief career could not be commemorated by the truth
as seen but by the truth as experienced by the psyche. Had
Alma lived in a simpler society, where the old are not useless
and unpopular, she would have had no trouble in commemo-
rating Cliff. In such a society it is the task of the aged to tell
the myths and reveal the secrets of religion and culture to the
young. She would have told the story of the nephew and it
would have been the story of the divine child.

This longing for Cliff was for the innocence of the Garden
of Eden, where the difference of good and evil was not known
and Eros was not denied. Cliff was the symbol of her own
suffering inner self with that hungry yearning which can
never be appeased. If she did not recognize Cliff while she
sheltered him, it was because the "guiltless," aloof from life,
know nothing. Only those who pay tribute to life and are
humbled by the awareness of their guilt can experience the
incarnation.

Now that Alma had renounced everything, the merciless
God of Job was still not through testing her. In quick night-
marish succession she received blow upon blow. A room in
her neighbor's house was on fire and in the blaze she saw a
row of life-sized photographs of Cliff strung across the room,
just as they were being consumed by the flames. How was it
that in a stranger's house there should be all these pictures

41

when she, the aunt, who cared for him more than anyone else had only a small, faded snapshot? Boyd had a heart attack and a telegram came from the War Department informing Miss Alma Mason that the death of her nephew had been definitely established. In the true tradition of the divine hero, his grave was unknown. "There should have been something left. . . . There should have been something from him for us."

With Boyd sick, she had to bear this final grief alone. "I have to think now of Boyd . . . . I can't afford not to be strong for him." The secret of Alma's strength at a time when so much affliction would have crushed anyone was that she could draw sustenance from two opposite sources: From the abiding love she had uncovered at the core of her being and from the disciplined, stoic world of her ancestors. "What you inherit from your father, must be regained," said Goethe. It is also true what we inherit from Mother must be recognized. Alma did both. The opposites within her were fusing and the schism healing. *Whatever was weak or querulous or unsure in Alma had gone, and only her strength was left.*

But still that implacable judge within her had tormenting questions. "Did the nephew love her?" For this answer she sought out Vernon Miller, Cliff's young friend, and begged him for the truth. "Cliff hated Rainbow," he told her. "He hated taking your and his uncle's charity . . . . He hated being without parents and thinking he was unwanted. He hated for you to feel you had to love him. He never wanted to come back here or to hear from anybody . . . . He was too proud to think anyone felt they wanted to love him. He thought nobody could love him or wanted him to stay with them."

"Didn't he know we loved him?" Alma cried.

"No Miss Mason," Vernon delivered the coup de grace. "He only knew he wanted to run off."

At this most crushing moment of her life, Alma answered with the dignity of the truly humble, "You told me the truth, and I believe it, but if you think I don't love Cliff all the more for hearing it, you're mistaken. Because I see how much more he needed the little love anyone could give. . . ."

Alma having renounced the rules and tradition that prevented her from loving, now had attained the highest ideal of all, of loving *the least among ye.*

She had now reached the depth of despair. The last blow, the most cruel of all, had beaten her to her knees. No human being is so strong that he has no breaking point, and this new knowledge imparted by Vernon Miller, was Alma's. She might never have gotten to her feet, had there not appeared at this moment a healing force, the counsel for defense, in the form of the sage Mrs. Barrington, with the other side of the truth. "Mrs. Barrington was, of course, the person one eventually had to see in Rainbow Center about anything of real importance."

"My nephew never loved me," Alma confessed to her defense counsel.

"You loved him, though, my dear," Mrs. Barrington bathed the wound. "And still do . . . . That's all we dare hope for in this life. . . . In your case, though you can hope for more. . . ."

Of Vernon's story, Mrs. Barrington said, "He told you the truth as he heard it, but it wasn't the truth as your nephew felt it. Your nephew loved you, and he loved Boyd. . . . And his wanting to run away, who doesn't want to run away from those they love, and at his age?"

In Boyd, who thanks to her ministrations recovered from his heart attack, she found another redeeming hand. Having grown old together and having shared this love for the nephew, they were now keenly sensitive to each other's needs. "You mustn't ever feel he didn't know," *she heard his voice coming to her as if out of some eternal darkness.* "Cliff knew we cared . . . . And that made him care too, at last, though he maybe never said it and he didn't have the gift . . . to write it."

By their practice of sitting in the dark, only their white
hair which at times shone almost like phosphorescence
betokened each other's presence.

Alma and Boyd were now Baucis and Philemon, the crones
of Phrygia, who opened their home to the divine wanderer
and were rewarded for their hospitality with a peaceful old
age together.

Cliff may not have had the gift to write of love, but this is
James Purdy's greatest gift of all. Alma said of her nephew,
"I never knew him, I only loved him." James Purdy shows us
that in her act of love, nonetheless, she knew all that one can
know of anyone.

MOTHER IS ALL!: *Children is All*

Stephen Dedalus in James Joyce's *A Portrait of the Artist as
a Young Man* defines tragedy as "whatsoever is grave and
constant in human sufferings." Engraved in human suffering
is the image that has come down to us from pre-history of the
mother holding her dying son in her arms — Michelangelo's
Pietà. Mythology and religion are full of wailing mothers
cradling their sacrificed sons, Tammuz, Attis, Adonis, Dyon-
isos or Christ. With the visions of the sorrowing mother hover-
ing over the dead carcass comes the memory that his death
was caused by her — that death came into the world through
woman. Medea wept while slaughtering her sons:

> I will not let them live for strangers to ill use
> To die by hands more merciless than mine?
> No, I who gave them life will give them death. *

James Purdy tells the eternal story of the Pietà. It is a tragic
poem in dialogue and is called *Children is All*.

* As quoted in *Mythology, Timeless Tales of Gods and Heroes* by Edith
Hamilton. Pages 129-130.

On an afternoon before the Fourth of July in a small town near Cairo, Illinois, "just outside the city limits," Edna is preparing for the homecoming of her son, Billy. He has been away for fifteen years in the state penitentiary on a bank embezzlement charge. For her the last fifteen years were "one long span." She has killed the fatted calf and is determined to receive the prodigal son well. "I've got to give out hope and gladness, and opportunity all at the same time," she vows. "Everything he didn't have where he's been I've got to give him here." Yet this passionately loving mother who shared his prison cell in spirit has not visited her son once in fifteen years. She explains, "And the few times I got my courage up to pay him a visit — once I got clear up to the prison gates — I couldn't go through with it! Oh I felt so bad to be such a weak thing. But I couldn't go past the iron gates . . . I felt if I went in, I would drop dead . . . ." But Hilda, a simple-minded girl of eighteen, visited Billy soon after she heard of his existence. Does she care more for Billy than his mother? "Shame in a kindred cannot be avoided," says an old proverb. Edna implicates herself still more when she talks of the trial.

> "I was so ashamed of myself that I didn't stay in court for the whole of it. Billy asked me to stay, so I would know the story, so he wouldn't be all alone with just accusers. . . . I fainted outside the witness room and was picked up and taken downstairs. . . ."

To abandon her boy to "just accusers" is deserting her young, as savages have done, to be devoured by wild beasts. In one of the most moving scenes of the play her pastor is trying to give her strength, and Edna sobs, "All I can think of is I will fail him. He will walk in and I will say, or show on my face: *The ex-convict has come home. I've opened my house to shame and disgrace.*"

The root meaning of shame is to "cover up," and in some languages it means "to wound." Edna's saying that she

45

opened her house to shame localizes the wound she wants to cover up. In dream language the house is the womb. The womb she once opened to fulfill its holy destiny, opened instead to whelp an embezzler, making her the mother of a criminal. ". . . ugly and slanderous to thy mother's womb" (*King John*). So great was her shame with its compulsion to hide from the public eye that when she had a chance to reopen the case by reason of new evidence, she failed her son again. At the same time she suffered from a private shame for having failed as a mother. Her self-esteem was completely shattered. She was a "weak thing," a failure. "I've found myself wanting where I should be strong. I'm deficient."

The awareness of her failure and her inability to rise above her shame make her a tragic figure. She knows she has Medea's bloody hands, and says with pathos, "Yes Billy carried the whole weight of the guilty, who ever was first responsible . . . . and such an inexperienced fellow to have to carry such a thing on top of him." The son's punishment for the sins of his elders, "who ever was first responsible," is another constant in human suffering. Every son is Christ.

On this long and agonizing day of Billy's homecoming, Edna's shame has given way to self-doubt, to mistrust, and finally to fear and panic. Her love had not been sufficient in the past, how sure could she be that if instead of making her son feel welcome she would not say those terrible words, "The ex-convict has come home . . . ." She sobs her anguish in biblical simplicity,

> "My fear is greater than I am. . . . It masters me by day
> and night. It seems to engulf all that I am, wherever
> I am. It blots out the world when it comes."

Her fear is justified — she is a murderess. At the beginning of the tragic poem Edna has sacrificed her son at the altar of the merciless goddess *Shame*, and at the end she puts a wreath of thorns on his bleeding brow when she doesn't recognize her wounded son on his return.

The need to be recognized is so urgent in Purdy's work that it is literally a matter of life and death. The recognition the son seeks lies in the definition of the word: To know again, to be acknowledged. Edna thought she heard her son's voice calling, "Be sure to recognize me now when I come home today, hear?" And Edna answers, "But Billy, how wouldn't I know my own flesh and blood?"

Billy asks to be *known again* and accepted for what he has become after fifteen years in prison, but Edna talks about *knowing* her flesh and blood, symbiotically — carnal knowledge, one might almost say. Billy's dying words are, "I only wanted you to recognize me before I go. I don't expect . . . anything more." But this recognition is the one thing Edna cannot give. She looks at the wounded stranger and says, "My son Billy was only a boy and you're a man . . . . You're all cut up."

In *Malcolm*, Madame Girard is the mother who wants to possess Malcolm as her very own. She sees him as "the idea of her life." When she comes to retrieve this object of her obsession from her would-be rival, she says, "I have only come here to claim my own." She never recognizes him as an individual with the right to grow away from her. True to the ambivalent nature of the eternal mother, she appears at Malcolm's deathbed. A moment before his death, Malcolm opens his eyes, and he cries, "It's not twenty years," referring to an appointment the undertaker, Estel Blanc, made with him. He has seen Medea, angel of death.

63: Dream Palace has the Pietà in fascinating juxtaposition. Claire's coffin is an old chest that contains a bridal veil — the womb. On the attic wall near the chest hangs a picture of a girl in a wedding dress, the eternally young owner of the womb turned tomb. There is also a framed poem concerning Mother Love and a picture of Christ among thieves. The

47

fourth picture of the young man in a hunting costume is a clue to the father missing in all the Pietà stories. He is the wanderer, the adventurer, who has forsaken his son on the *golden bench of Malcolm* and is not there to protect him from the devouring mother and thieves.

In "Eventide," Mahala the Negro mother cannot believe that her son Teeboy has left her. Her sister Plumy reports the devastating fact that Teeboy has straightened his hair, and Mahala comes to the sad conclusion, "Until you told me about his having his hair straightened, I thought maybe he would be back." She knows only the woolly-haired infant still warm and moist from her womb and amniotic fluid. Her craving body cannot understand the wisdom of Ecclesiastes: "For everything there is a season . . . a time to embrace and a time to refrain from embracing."

Grieving over her loss, Mahala becomes envious of her sister whose son died at the age of four. "Somehow the idea of George Watson being dead so long and yet still being a baby a mother could love had a kind of perfect quality that she liked. She thought then, quietly and without shame, how nice it would be if Teeboy could also be perfect in death, so that he would belong to her in the same perfect way as George Watson belonged to Plumy." In her fantasy she is the eternal mother united with her son in death — *the perfect quality* of the Pietà.

In "Why Can't They Tell You Why?" the mother is as terrifying as the witch in Hansel and Gretel. We witness the ritual murder itself, undisguised, undistilled. The little boy stares at his mother as she opens the door of the furnace and we see her with him, ". . . as though all the nightmares had come true, the complete and final fear of what may happen in living had unfolded itself at last."

Nera, the aged mother in "Cracks," looks over the distance of times that removed her from the scene of her maternal crime and sums up with terrible clarity all that is grave and constant in human suffering when she says of her dead children, "We destroy our own gifts one by one."

In the Greek myth, Jocasta is the mother who cannot recognize her son and this blindness has made her *the* symbol of the incestuous mother — queen of hell, whose kiss spelled death.

In Michelangelo's Pietà, the beautiful young mother looking serene and fulfilled betrays no physical strain such as the dead weight of a grown man would realistically give her. It is as if she carried an infant on her lap instead.

Edna as she cleans the head wound of her unrecognized thirty-three year old son (the age of Christ) is reliving the time when she took care of her child. "When Billy was a baby, he so often fell and got hurt. . . . I used to take my pocket handkerchief . . . and I would moisten it with my . . . spit." She is the young mother of the Pietà.

When Billy dies in her lap, she says, "I feel I almost welcomed him home and put him to sleep, as calm as if I'd been. . . ." And then she continues, "I feel so close to my son," as close as when she first knew him as a part of her body. She is the Madonna, serenely cradling her son's hand in her own, in the "kind of perfection" that Mahala yearned for.

Edna is holding her dead son in her arms and her mind has mercifully lost its hold on impossible, unbearable reality. "The knot that held her together all these years is broken." Mother and son so cruelly hit by "the slings and arrows of outrageous fortune" (*Hamlet*) have found release in insanity and death. No longer will they have to endure the wounds of shame, the hunger for recognition and "whatsoever is grave and constant in human suffering."

With terror and pity, love, hate, and grief, James Purdy portrays the mother whose life is dominated by her biology, her womb; the woman who is unable to part with her offspring and cannot recognize his right to reach manhood. It is her destiny to nourish the fetus with her body from the moment of conception only to have to expel the child and start it on its chilly road to death. Both mother and child are scarred by this experience and James Purdy reveals these mortal scars unsparingly.

LOVE IN THE TWENTIETH CENTURY:
Cabot Wright Begins

James Purdy's work is about love. Love between mother and child, brother and brother or sister, husband and wife, aunt and nephew, friends, neighbors, strangers. People stumbling, groping towards each other, and failing. Always failing cruelly, tragically, when the very survival of the beloved depends on love. Why our way of loving cannot stand the test becomes clear in "Man and Wife." Lafe, the "man" of the story, tries to explain to the fat Peaches Maud the reason he was fired from the factory job "in good times," but she won't listen. He says, turning white, "You never let me show you nothing but the outside" to which she shouts, "Well that's all anybody human wants to hear."

From early childhood on we are taught to feel guilty and ashamed of our *inside*, and so we cultivate a façade. What we call love is often one façade falling for another façade. Yet in the *inside*, in our central experience, is all human reality. In James Purdy's stories, the need to be recognized and accepted for one's *inside* is so desperate that his characters cannot live without it. Without the recognition of their human reality they themselves do not know who they are. This puts them at the mercy of everyone's whims and finally destroys them. "Love is possible only if two persons communicate with each other from the center of their existence," as Erich Fromm expresses it in *The Art of Loving*.

The inability to communicate from this center pervades all of Purdy's work. Beyond this universal failure each epoch has its own reason for failing. And what the Twentieth century imprint is, the author tells us in *Cabot Wright Begins*.

It is the story of rape from our human heritage, as devastating as Huxley's *Brave New World*; more alarming because it is not a prediction of things to come but of how in our lifetime we have been turned into robots and drug addicts for easier manipulation by money and power. Robots and drug addicts cannot love; they can be conditioned to go through the motions but not the emotions. Cabot Wright, the protagonist, "after having been born anesthetic from the womb" and placed into a strange nest, is as disconnected from our human past as Huxley's test-tube babies. He asks while groping for his memory, "Where is the keenest place you can hurt a man?" Then he answers his own question, "Not in the eye or groin but where he can't remember." Without a memory he cannot know who he is. He can only buy the personality hawked to him by Madison Avenue. He has nothing left of his own — not even a choice. Robots cannot choose. When the young, drug-addicted robots protest it is not against the order of things but for the latest in chemically induced kicks.

"All effective propaganda," Hitler wrote, "must be confined to a few stereotyped formulas." These stereotyped formulas must be constantly repeated for "only constant repetition will finally succeed in imprinting an idea upon the memory of the crowd."

Young Cabot Wright grew up in an era when America was ruled by stereotyped formulas, repeated, not by a political dictator, of course, but by commercial propagandists with even more efficient and advanced technical and scientific methods at their command. To turn unpredictable humans into predictable mass consumers with standardized tastes they exploit secret fears and hopes and cravings, anxieties and frustrations — a method proved so effective in Nazi Germany.

What are the formulas that control Cabot Wright? James Purdy, with the diabolical humor of the outraged, portrays

Dr. Bugleford, a psychotherapist of the modern Procrustes school, dedicated to adjusting everyone to the size of the Hollywood double bed. He has his group therapy "Marriage — or — Death" class shout in chorus:

I WILL MARRY, MARRY, MARRY & WILL PLAY SAFE PLAY SAFE AND OBEY. WE'LL BE MISTER AND MRS. O.K. O.K. THANKS TO THAT INSTITU-TION THAT MAKES ME GO & SOCIETY HUM, OVER-ALL INSTITUTION! HETEROSEX FOUNT OF PROGRESS AND FUN! MARRIAGE! MARRIAGE! MARRIAGE! MARRIAGE CAN BE FUN! I WILL MARRY! HETEROSEX! FUN! MONEY, MONEY, HETEROSEX FUN! I WILL MARRY! OBEY! OBEY! OBEY! FUN! HETEROSEX! LIFE INSURANCE! LIFE! HETEROSEX MARRIAGE! INSURANCE!

Cabot Wright obeys, plays safe, marries and *has fun*. Having fun, he has been taught, is his duty if not purpose in life, and consists of consuming and taking in. I BOUGHT IT GOD I BOUGHT IT AND IT'S GREAT IT'S HOLLY-WOOD. . . . Cabot Wright and Cynthia, his wife, are so patriotic in the pursuit of fun, that their sizeable joint income plus support by a rich father cannot pay the bill, and like the rest of "buy-now-pay-later America" they are deeply in debt.

"Where does the money go?" came so frequently from her mouth that Cabot pinned the words, cut from an advertisement, on the wall above their dinette.

Cynthia, who can only speak in the metallic slogans hammered out by Public Relations, finally asks, "Do you love me?" And the young husband true to his mass media conditioning answers, "I adore it." This shortest of dialogue sums up the disintegration of love in our time, where it has come to mean *it*, impersonal sex, and nothing else.

Mr. and Mrs. Cabot Wright, Jr., are the young marrieds of the 1960's. For the parents responsible for these anesthetized post-war boom babies, James Purdy paints a portrait of the middle-aged Carrie Moore and fourth husband Bernie Gladhart, the depression children of the second quarter of the century.

> Carrie had grown up in an age which practiced promiscuous coitus as an injunction, if not duty. Marriage, she and her contemporaries felt, was easier and more sensible than the single state, though not laudable or noticably rewarding in itself — a gray *faute de miex.*

In an outrageously funny paragraph the author evokes a devastating image of "coitus as an injunction."

> Every night at 9:15 p.m., Bernie mounted the winding staircase, in his dressing-robe, to Carrie's huge bedroom at the top of the landing, and for fifteen interminable minutes, man and wife thrashed vigorously together among the bedclothes. . . . Bernie, battling to keep his virile member belligerent, fought out the quarter hour, until his wife's cries signalled success; then he retired from the fray without having spilled a drop of himself, keeping what he had bottled up, as it were for the exigencies of the next night. . . . She never insisted outright that he reach consummation with her, for vigor, not self-satisfaction, were the requisites she asked of her husband.

Bernie drifted into marriage because he longed for shelter, and Carrie's alimony house from an ex-husband ironically gave him a "holy feeling . . . an at home feeling of belonging." In return for his daily 9:15 p.m. stint, Carrie — good teammate that she was — gives her husband "encouragement and praise by the wagonload . . . and a becalming feeling supported at every level."

Love as coitus by injunction, as teamwork, and as an *at*

home feeling of belonging is a far cry from communicating from the center of one's existence.

Much has been said and written about the phallic woman to whom equality means to be the same as man. James Purdy in one short sentence instinctively pinpoints the malaise of the Twentieth century woman: "She had half-starved her own daughter in infancy," he tells us of Carrie Moore. A woman who half-starves her infant daughter totally rejects her own feminine identity. She is of the generation that found breast feeding too repulsive, domesticated, and enslaving. The first taste and suckling sensation she offered her infant, born drugged to spare the mother the pains of birth, was from a new-improved synthetic rubber nipple on a glass bottle, propped up and thrust into the rooting mouth at scheduled intervals. What did Carrie Moore save her breast for?

> Waiting for evening, dressed only in her foundation but with her wired bra lifted to dizzy heights, she snuggled under a coverlet. . . .

The stiffly erect position into which the breasts were pushed is the one position in which they could not be of the smallest use or comfort to the suckling babe, or of delight to the lover. Carrie Moore has become emancipated from womanhood. The sexual polarities have been destroyed and erotic love, being based on these polarities, has disappeared with it.

Love as teamwork, advocated by the marriage efficiency experts, depends on proximity, and when Bernie Gladhart is banished by Carrie to the "cold-sea fog city" of Brooklyn in search of material for a book she insists he must write, she at once finds another lover for her *wedding bower*. "The two clasped each other like stars before a cameraman who had shot this scene innumerable times before."

In this cold climate of anti-love, anti-sex, anti-life, where people use and destroy each other, there is one scene, "like the one warm spark in the heart of an arctic crystal" (Melville).

This scene, reminiscent of the meeting of Ishmael and Queequeg, dramatizes the same yearning for simplicity and innocence.

Bernie Gladhart, like Ishmael, is the homeless outsider and dreamer — the only American not yet "glutted without knowing the feeling of either hunger or satiety." The only American open to love. Finding himself isolated in Brooklyn, dejected enough to think of looking for trouble, he sees a tall African. "The man walked like a prince and was obviously not impressed by anything except what was inside." Bernie saw ". . . an Ideal Man, and in his desperation and yet stubborn mood, decided to love him." Bernie Gladhart, a failure by the standards of our society, is the only one who knows that love is a decision — a decision to embrace the core of another human being. It is a love that can only hope for reciprocation — but it asks for no such guarantee. It is a love that does not *play safe*, risking rejection and ostracism.

Winters Hart, the princely man of the Congo, too, found himself isolated, "in a racial democracy," as he confided to Bernie. "You can keep Black America . . . . if it means working all day to turn white." After exchanging the necessary information about themselves, the two isolates immediately communicate with each other from the core. Bernie disarmingly says, "I hope this will be as deeply a felt relationship for you as it is for me." And Winters Hart answers, "Americans always explain me how they're doing a right thing . . . but no need to celebrate it by way of explanations." Bernie sleeps spoon-fashion, next to the heart of his Congolese friend and it soothes him. For the first time this orphaned child feels human warmth. He can go on again.

When this scene is contrasted with the harsh separation of husband and wife, the moment Carrie's *cries signalled success*, it becomes clear what the sex-obsessed propagandists of the mass media omit: the need for spontaneous warmth and affection. The institutionalized child that cannot survive without the human and loving touch is still very much alive and yearning in Bernie Gladhart. Carrie's wired breast offered no tenderness to this half-starved child.

For the first generation of the Twentieth century, the spiritual parents of Carrie Moore, James Purdy draws a lively, affectionate though unsparing portrait of Mr. and Mrs. Warburton. "Mr. Warburton, who dated from the Great Days of Wall Street, was continuously depressed at the way things were going downhill." His world was being destroyed before his eyes. "I've always been satisfied with basing my life on making a fortune and centering myself around the System," he says, "but today I'm surrounded by men and women whom *nothing* can satisfy one way or another." And now he looked at the world he helped create with his Nineteenth century materialism and he felt, "wrath, indignation, hatred, loathing, distaste, weariness, ennui, nausea, surfeit, and animadversion that expressed itself in diatribes against all and everybody, including himself."

Mr. Warburton's awareness and his passion expressed in an earthy vocabulary, untouched by pre-fab phrases, make him an individual in an anti-individual society. He is still alive. He gives his bored young general partner, Cabot Wright, the feeling that "for the first time in life he was actually talking with another human being about something." Mr. Warburton is angry because Cabot Wright and his generation are always tired. He remembers in his day no one was tired. What the old Puritan inherited from his forebears was a love for work and discipline, if nothing else. Why did he fail in handing down these virtues that founded America? Love for one's work has little meaning at a time when enterprises are so vastly centralized that man loses his individuality. He becomes a cog in the wheel, an appendage to a machine. Cabot says, "My life is largely paper work." How can he not be tired and bored? In Mr. Warburton's youth it was possible, with a little capital and hard work, to build up a business of one's own. This led to incentive and pride in personal achievement. That time has passed. It was inevitable. The fault for this cannot be laid at Mr. Warburton's feet. Where he is at fault is that he limited his love to work alone, excluding human beings. Had he taught his children and grandchildren to love life itself, to hold dear the essence of the human, they would not so easily have become the foil of the mind manipulators who thrive on the absence of this love, and on the absence of recognition of the inner self.

Gilda Warburton, the wife of the great financier, is ". . . a woman of indeterminate age, much younger than her spouse, with a popular wig of the hour, a breast alight with jewels . . . and a stale dank gin breath."

"How would one describe my life. . . ." she asks. "Dressing up and getting there takes the day." In Mr. Warburton's world she is the hostess. He tells her in his Nineteenth century male arrogance, "I regard this as my hotel . . . in point of fact, and a damned good one it is, too." She answers, "You have brought more vacuum in places I had no idea existed." This unrealized woman, parasitically depending on others to fill her vacuum, tries to add a little color to her monotonous life. Color comes in the form of a TV set and a Negro butler with whom she consorts. This Alabama-bred lady wants to stay abreast of a time she cannot possibly comprehend. In a devilish, satirical monologue she says of the civil rights struggle, "I feel deeply close to this wonderful new awakening nation within us. . . . Our sterling friends, noble people with a great tomorrow."

It is from this unfulfilled life of the kept wife that Carrie Moore rebelled so violently and found expression in "promiscuous coitus as an injunction." This too was inevitable. But sex as a form of rebellion can have very little meaning for the next generation whose battle is already won. One may assume that between the extremes of Victorianism and Carrie Moore-ism, the new generation would have struck a balance, had not the advertisers gotten into the act and made "promiscuous coitus an injunction if not duty" for everyone, leaving desires for love, union, and closeness unfulfilled. In Mr. Warburton's pungent, outrageous vocabulary, "It's the time when the country has less virility than ever before . . . and the whole communication media devoted to sex-unsex. All America talks of nothing but sex . . . and there isn't a stiff pecker or a warm box in the house."

James Purdy's vision of horror is not without faith in humanity. *Cabot Wright Begins* is essentially the story of Cabot trying to cure himself of what the world made him. His cure, his rebirth as human comes with laughter. "After all, laughter is the greatest boon Nature has bestowed on miserable unjoyous man." Cabot concludes movingly, testifying to man's endurance, "I thought I'd die but I lived."

AT THE DUGS OF SAVAGE TIGERS:
Eustace Chisholm and the Works

I know thee, Love! in deserts thou wert bred,
And at the dugs of savage Tigers fed;
Alien of birth, usurper of the plains!
                                        — Virgil*

At one point in *Eustace Chisholm and the Works*, the mother of the young hero, Amos Ratcliffe, starts to confide to her best friend, "a most unwelcome subject," the incestuous love-act that led to her son's exile. This is more than Lily, the friend, can endure and she warns, "Don't tell me. Certain secrets a woman must keep buried in her own heart. . . . We have to carry some things with us to the grave. . . ."

But human beings are not made to keep secrets. "What we try to conceal oozes from our pores." (Freud) The oozing se-

* As translated by Dryden and quoted by James Purdy in *Eustace Chisholm and the Works.*

crets in this tragic, violent, and tender love-story are so crystallized and enacted that it's impossible to join Lily in turning away, though we wish we could. They corner us like dreams at night when we come face to face with a "most unwelcome subject," our innner self.

James Purdy tells the story of Daniel Haws, torn between two jealous gods, the innate human conscience that demands fulfillment through love, and the imposed authoritarian conscience that makes love an abomination when Cupid's careless arrows pierce the "wrong" two hearts and souls. Obeying one god means violating the laws of the other. Daniel Haws must choose between the hell of self-rejection and ostracism by the world. Either alternative is a punishment far greater than man can bear. It's the agony of civilized man.

Daniel Haws, who runs a rooming house in Chicago during the depression, secretly loves his young boarder, Amos Ratcliffe. This rugged ex-soldier, clinging to the order and discipline of the army with the compulsion of his Puritan forebears, conceals this secret even from himself. The only time Daniel's love cannot be silenced is in his sleep:

> Awake, he not only never made a single pass at Amos Ratcliffe, but seemed to keep a gulf between them all the time. . . . [Amos] knew that . . . a sleepwalker wearing Daniel Haws' face and body, but with a different soul, would visit him in his cubicle, smooth his hair, mumble words of blind affection. . . .

Amos Ratcliffe was seventeen and beautiful. But it was not merely youth and beauty that made Daniel, who up to this time (twenty-five years of age), had given full expression to his heterosexual leanings, fall "head over heels" with a boy. Daniel scrubbed himself clean "as only a man who hates himself can. . . ." and was no sensualist, no pleasure seeker. He was ascetic, austere. Whether it was the strain of Indian blood mixed with the Puritan that played havoc or whether all men are born with pagan blood that asserts itself when least expected, in any event there was something about Amos Ratcliffe that made Daniel "boy sick."

Amos Ratcliffe has the quality of a pagan love god: Springtime fresh, "immune to evil customs," mischievous as Pan, and without a sense of guilt for natural impulses. He has whatever was once spontaneous and childlike in us and has been destroyed by civilization. If these qualities made Daniel sick with longing for a childhood only his Indian blood recalled, it was Daniel who made Amos "father sick."

Amos Ratcliffe, *the beautiful bastard* "brought up more lovingly than an heir," needed a father. From his mother, Cousin Ida, he received the love of a savage tigress for her cub. It was so natural and unconscious that Amos was not even aware she was his mother and that there were rules in the world outside "the frilled snowy curtains behind the tiny windows," that forbade a son to embrace his mother sexually. The shock of consciousness catapulted him into exile — into the manmade world where the laws of the natural world were not acceptable and would destroy him.

What Amos needs from Daniel is to soak up his masculinity and absorb the traits necessary to survive in the civilized world. (A point of orientation, knowledge and adaptability to law and mores, self-discipline and an ability to support himself.) These are the gifts Daniel has to offer. Ironically, Daniel's standards of masculinity, so admired by Amos, forbid him to give anything to a boy that might be taken for affection and deep interest. Daniel's male pride, prudence, and industriousness, now become a means of escape from facing his fear of love.

As much as Amos needs Daniel's adaptability to the outer world Daniel needs Amos's acceptance of the inner world. Daniel's reaching blindly for Amos transcends physical need. Something from his very depth is seeking completion. The failure to achieve this total unfolding proves catastrophic.

Daniel is beset by many symptoms that reveal his inner suffering — sudden rages, an inability to look the boy in the eye, unsteady hand, unaccountable feeling of terror, and a slip of tongue calling Amos "Kewpie" — Cupid. But he ignores all the symptoms. His ego will not let him admit that he no longer is in control of his life. Instead, he goes to great lengths to repress his love. But this force cannot be stemmed and keeps streaming through him. What could have been a creative well-spring of life had it been acknowledged and responsibly directed, now turns into a poisonous secretion that oozes out. This is what Eustace Chisholm, the friend gifted with second sight, means when he calls love the "poisoned cup." The love potion that drips from a leak and is handed to Amos at night by a sleepwalker, is poison to the boy who already had been ruined by blind, castrating mother love. "I'm just real enough for a sleepwalker to love," he says beyond despair. To be looked at and not seen, to be touched and not felt, to be talked to without the speaker hearing his own words of affection stretch the boy's feeling of insignificance and isolation to the point of madness. The only antidote for the poisoner and poisoned would be recognition and action that did not violate the integrity of either.

Everything in the story builds up with dreadful foreboding to the inevitable moment of truth when Daniel is cornered and must face his sleepwalking self. When lightning struck, *the scaffolding of his life fell*:

> — He could not feel he wanted the body of Amos . . . but he could not deny to himself in his hours of blinding self-revelation that he needed Amos, that it was Amos who dictated everything he felt and represented all he needed. That his whole being was now taken up with a mere boy was simply the last of the long series of disasters which had been his life.
>
> — Ever a victim of melancholy . . . he reached the depth

of his hell. And all the while only the remembrance of Amos's fair face held him even to a breath of hope.

Amos, nature's child, becomes the usurper of Daniel's whole being. But even then, he cannot accept the boy. The stern voice within forbids it. When his former girl-friend, Maureen O'Dell, asks why he can't admit his love to Amos, to whom such a confession means life itself, Daniel shoots back, "Why don't you ask God?" Was he referring to the wrathful God of Calvin and the Puritans, who denied the supreme role of love? This God does not exist in the religious sense to Daniel; nevertheless He has been internalized and Daniel is His slave.

Daniel finds himself now cast in an age-old role — that of the father forsaking his son, thus forsaking himself. "Whatever we do to others we do to ourselves," is the existential theme in Purdy's work. When Amos in his desperate struggle for survival receives an offer from a middle-aged millionaire playboy to keep him, Daniel does not lift a finger to prevent the youth from accepting. In the crucial scene of the book, Amos pleads, "Tell me not to, and I won't."

> Expecting something definite from Daniel, a defiant "no" or a blow from his fists, the landlord's "go" was the last of crushed hopes and disappointments for Amos, who stood now, his eyes beginning to fill.

There is a déjà vu feeling in this scene. Amos has accompanied Maureen O'Dell, who once loved Daniel and was made pregnant by him, to an illegal, crudely performed abortion:

> Amos's eyes strayed to the open garbage can, and he pondered that there lay Daniel Haws's son, the proof of his manhood.

Amos who had not been accepted by his own father, then is abandoned again by Daniel, has as little chance as the

62

discarded "battered and decapitated fetus" in the open garbage can.

Daniel seals his own fate with the betrayal. "I failed him as I failed myself." No court of justice metes out punishment for crimes against one's self. It is a merciless, cruel inner judge that punishes such violations.

The scaffolding of Daniel's life having fallen, he seeks the order and protection of the army. Eustace Chisholm, who knows everything by reason of second sight and serves as a Greek chorus, predicts, "The army is not going to be a Mother to you, but your dark bridegroom." Where Daniel's conscious reason seeks refuge, his unconscious one manifests itself immediately. He sleepwalks naked into his captain's tent, summoning him to be his judge and executioner. Ever the Puritan, Daniel confronts his judge without an advocate, hoping to be broken into complete submission. As he expresses it in a letter to Eustace Chisholm:

> I am under, I understand, a Captain Stadger, who is death in circles, and I hear from beforehand he will exercise all the authority he has over me, well, let him, let him put me on the wheel if he has to and twist until I recognize the authority of the army so good there will be nothing but it over me, over and above Amos and even all the pain. . . .

But submission will not come and the memory of Amos will not leave. There ensues a titanic conflict between the two jealous gods. Stadger speaks for the outraged authoritarian conscience and the Amos within Daniel represents the human conscience. Daniel and Stadger find themselves locked in a climactic ceremonial act from which neither knows how to escape. They are shackled together in a symbiotic union, one completely dependent on the other, each losing the integrity of his individual self. Stadger is obviously the persecutor, but he is just as much a victim as Daniel. When caught unaware

63

he looks youthful and innocent like Amos. The moment he relents his torture, Daniel prods him back to his assigned role.

Captain Stadger as judge and executioner hounds, punches, and slashes Daniel to make him deny and profane his love. Yet Daniel will not yield. Neither can he be made to confess his love to Amos directly — thus he yields not to Cupid either. He is hopelessly deadlocked, ". . . he had come to that limit of life where no action on one's own part is possible or thinkable." He can neither commit himself to one side or the other, nor can he reconcile the two. This paralysis of the will is the existential guilt corroding his soul.

Captain Stadger is now driven by a mad obsession to get at the nucleus of Daniel and extract that certain something that made him at once welcome the torture and resist it:

> "You give only resistance while yielding. Against your granite then I've got to find a substitute. I've got to make your hardness yield to some other hardness which I'll have to bring from the outside. Now we've gone this far, neither of us can stop until you give me complete submission."

The torture he inflicts on Daniel transcends sadism. It is motivated by something deeper, the wish to get at Daniel's treasure — the secret of his life. "Burglars use diamond-tipped drills to get at their treasure. . . ." But the more he drills into the depth of Daniel's being, the more the secret eludes him. Desperately, he tries to gain complete power over Daniel, ". . . he had everything *on* him and from him, and he carried his whole life with him as no other person living or dead could or ever had. . . ." But the secret cannot be tortured out of Daniel.

Daniel exults in the torture. He welcomes the pain for his betrayal and at the same time he wants to die and be free of the burdensome, unasked-for treasure. *He had never wanted to be alive.* But in spite of this passionate longing for death, his mouth pronounces the life-affirming secret, "Amos." When he had been near Amos, it was ". . . the only time he had ever been alive." This is the secret Stadger cannot grasp. He cannot understand that life and love are one. This insight can never be gained through an act of destruction. Stadger's consuming passion for Daniel's secret and his self-defeating action make him human and tragic.

Before the final belaboring with torture instruments, Captain Stadger gives Daniel his last chance. He thrusts a photograph of Amos in front of his victim and says, "Prefer me to him now, and you're free, Haws." The jealous "dark bridegroom" is losing the match to Eros, and as a last desperate measure he resorts to blackmail. Daniel does not yield.

All Stadger can attack is the *compact of blood, bone, flesh*. Even when he disembowls Daniel, Eros cannot be dislodged. Having failed in his life's mission, there is only one thing left to do for Captain Stadger — shoot himself.

The symbiotic tie to the deadly authoritarian part of Daniel is destroyed. "I have stood all tests" are his final words.

Daniel Haws is James Purdy's most tragic character. He hates himself, he hates life, and yet alongside this hatred there exists a passionate striving for love. He cannot accept this striving, and the insoluble conflict tears him to shreds. The same man who *cannot* admit his love to Amos, *can* stand all tests rather than denounce it.

"What a piece of work is a man!" (Hamlet).